AROUND PUCKLECHURCH – THEN

by IAN S. BISHOP

INTRODUCTION

In this, the third book in my Then and Now series, I have taken an area which was originally part of the manor of Pucklechurch, and includes Westerleigh in the North to Wick in the South, plus Shortwood; Abson; Doynton, and Dyrham. The districts covered are areas which over the centuries have been linked together, as they form a cluster of communities at the base of The Southwolds.

The name Pucklechurch has no significant religious connotations but, instead, it is believed to have been derived and/or corrupted from two Saxon words meaning 'fair', and 'down'. During this time, Pucklechurch stood at the edge of a great Royal hunting forest and was the site of a King's Palace although, today, it would be regarded as nothing more than a large wooden hall, where much feasting and debauchery took place. It was, in fact, during one of these events in the year 946 AD, that the Saxon King Edmund 1 was stabbed to death whilst fighting with an outlaw by the name of Leolf or Liulph. The reputed site of the Palace is now covered by a Farmhouse situated behind the Star Inn. Edmund's body was conveyed to the religious centre of Glastonbury for burial and so that masses could be said for his soul. It is possibly for this reason that in return the Manor of Pucklechurch was given to the Abbey of Glastonbury. Certainly the whole of the manor, including Westerleigh, Abson and Wick appear in the Domesday Book as part of Glastonbury under the name of Pulcrecerce.

Of some of the other places visited in this book, Westerleigh obtained its name from the fact that it was a settlement in the lee of the western extremity of the surrounding uplands, and this community probably started around open pasture land, although later coal and iron were both mined. Abson is a corruption of Abbots/ton i.e. a place belonging to the Abbot whilst Wick was for a considerable time a large source of iron products, with the local carboniferous rocks also containing quantities of coal and iron. More recently Wick was famous for producing fuller's earth, ochres and oxide colours. By 1912, the Golden Valley Ochre & Oxide Company was employing at least 100 men.

Whilst many of the pictures reproduced in this book have been taken from the author's collection, I am indebted to Mike Tozer for providing additional and interesting views to be shared with the reader. My special thanks go to my wife Doreen for helping me match-up the Now pictures, and for her continued support in producing this record.

August 1998   Ian S. Bishop

Westerleigh Tabernacle built in 1844, and three cottages on the narrow quiet country road leading to Rodford, and on to Nibley, around 1904, with family group on extreme right posing for the camera. This card was used as a New Year's greeting, having been posted on the 30 December 1905, with a message containing the phrase "the girl on here is our Alice" signed M. Webb.

A pavement now replaces the grass verge, and the road has been widened, and surfaced to cope with today's traffic requirements. The building on the left is now the Grace Evangelical Church, with the Rodford Tabernacle behind. Across the skyline stretches the modern source of power on towering ungainly pylons. Elm Farm is in the background.

The Village Grocers/Drapers shop around 1910 when owned by H. Underwood & Co., who also have a depot at Frampton Cotterell. Six young children and, possibly Mr. Underwood himself have been arranged by the photographer, whilst the tower of St. James the Great rises majestically above the village.

George Ruff & Son now run the shop and, whilst it is no longer a drapers, it has been adapted to become a newsagents, as well as the Village Post Office. Little appears to have changed to the exterior of the building, although the left-hand chimney stack has been shortened. To the right of the shop a modern telephone box has been installed.

639. CPC   Westerleigh, from Railway Bridge

Looking along the un-named road towards the centre of the village, with the Early English Perpendicular tower of St. James the Great gazing down on the *'Kings Arms'* and the Mill House Farm. The cameraman has gathered a rather self-conscious young man who views the event with curious interest not realising that that moment would be frozen in time. c.1910.

The railway bridge and its supporting wall are extant, but the left-hand grass verge has given way to a sensible pavement, which in turn has helped the road to be modernized to meet the strenuous demands of todays traffic. On the right-hand side, most of the fields/paddocks have given way to houses as more and more people move into the village.

WESTERLEIGH.

Further along the same road during a bright sunny summer afternoon in the early 1950's. A small group stand in position for the cameraman. Behind them is the Oak House, and rising above the property are the distinctive lines of the lofty, embattled church tower, which contains a clock and six bells.

Old Mill Close has now been constructed on the right, whilst the trees have grown much larger shielding the view of the semi-detached houses on the left. This once quiet and peaceful road is now a busy thoroughfare, as partly demonstrated by the seven cars in the picture.

SHORTWOOD, PUCKLECHURCH.

44165

Looking along Main Road, at Shortwood some time during the early 1950's. Five young men group together to watch the antics of the cameraman, whilst the road is occupied not by cars, but by just two cyclists.

With the increasing importance of owning cars in the 1990's, many of the garden walls have been breached to make way for parking spaces, whilst other vehicles pass them by as they busy themselves through the chicanes of life.

Siston, Near Mangotsfield. No. 178.

T.H.S. & CO. B. & C.

St. Anne's Bridge carrying Syston Lane over Syston Brook, with the trees from Hanging Wood reaching down to the roadside. On the right behind the foliage is the pond and weir which form part of St. Anne's Well. c.1910. Historically, the spelling of Syston has always been as shown, but it is now officially spelt Siston.

The side-wall of the bridge has been partially re-built, and the road has been designed to occupy as much of the space as possible. No longer is Siston Lane a quiet country byway, with more and more vehicles vying for the narrow space which makes it uncomfortable for cars to pass each other. The area once occupied by the pond is now overgrown with summer vegetation.

St. Anne's Church nestles amongst the trees, with the hamlet of Syston off to the right. The church is an ancient building of stone in the Norman style, with a western tower topped with four ornate pinnacles and serves the parish of Syston, the bulk of which stretches away to the West. This picture was probably taken around 1912 and was posted on the 16 March 1916.

The reposeful scene, as depicted in the adjoining picture has been lost in the passage of time, as have the attractive pinnacles and stone balustrade that once adorned the top of the tower. Unfortunately, their loss has meant that the church has given up some of its beauty and charm, as it watches over the motorized traffic hurrying by.

Along Shortwood Road are old folks bungalows newly built on the 'out-skirts' of Pucklechurch, as the housing stock of the area begins its post-war expansion to accommodate the influx of people moving out from the central city areas. c.1967.

Little appears to have changed to this part of the village over the past thirty years, the roadside is now much tidier following the clearance of the builders' rubble; street signs have been erected and, for once, the main road is free of traffic, although probably not for long.

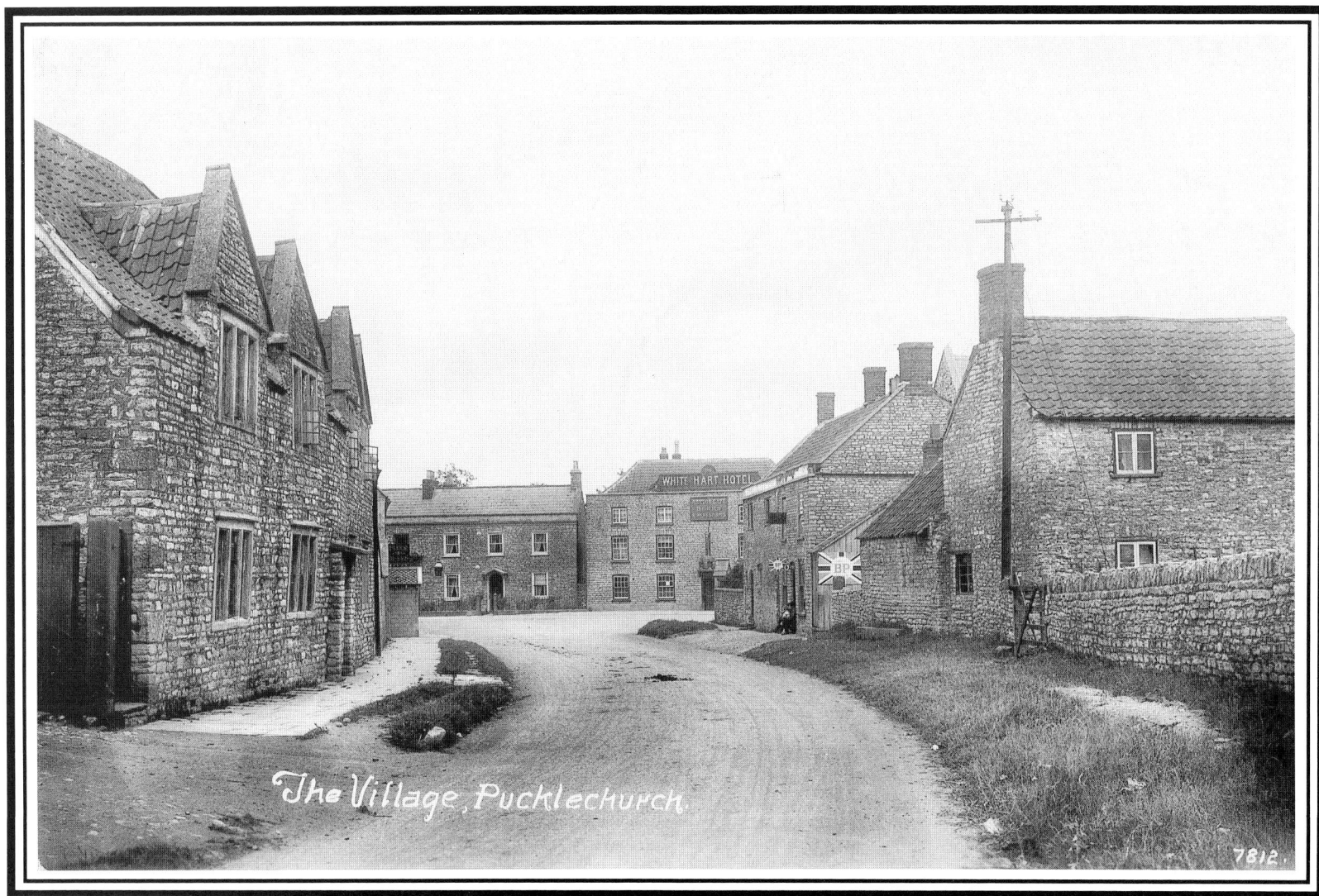

The Village, Pucklechurch.

7812.

Shortwood Road around 1925. Despite the introduction of asphalt, the poor pedestrian was still expected to walk through the grass or run the risk of being knocked over by horse powered traffic of both kinds. At the cycle shop, the fledgling British Petroleum Company is trying to get a foothold in the village. Ashton Gate Beer Wines and Spirits can be obtained from *The White Hart.*

The motorized traffic has won the day and now predominates most of village life. Newspapers and magazines are sold where once Farnham Dury made cycles, whilst alcoholic drinks can, in this area, only be consumed on the premises of the *Fleur de Lys.* Apart from the development of new buildings to the right of the camera, most of the property in the picture remains structurally the same.

The *Fleur de Lys* in the centre of the village during the mid 1960's, with nobody about. Courages have taken over Georges Bristol Brewery and that upstart lager, as per the 'Harp' advert, is beginning to challenge the mild and bitter brigade.

Little appears to have changed to the external appearance of the *Fleur de Lys* over the past thirty-five years or so, but no doubt there have been many changes within. In the meanwhile, the property on the right has now been converted into a house.

The hub of the village showing the area on the same quiet summers day, as depicted in the cover picture. The cart-horse still awaits patiently his master's return from the Hotel. A villager is unsteady on one of those new-fangled bicycles, whilst a young man stands outside Dr. Legats surgery. Although the picture was taken around 1910, the card was not postally used until 13 October 1943.

No longer the peaceful hub of the village, but the centre of much activity and congestion. Although the buildings are still there, unlike the opposite view, there is no Hotel or Doctor's surgery to attend. The intricate and decorative pediment which once adorned the village shop has now given way to the sharper edges of a modern facade. Wires and posts add to the general clutter.

Parkfield Road from the Village Green, with the Moat House built in 1857 on the left. Again there are no proper pavements to help the pedestrian on his/her way, although by the look of the path across the top of the bank, many feet have made quite an impression. A young girl with three younger children, help to turn this into a charming rural picture of Pucklechurch around 1910.

The roadway has been re-surfaced and had its edges curbed whilst, alongside, the earth bank has given way to a more convenient pavement to meet the demands of the 1990's, which appear to include the parking of cars, as guests attend a wedding at the nearby St. Thomas the Martyr. Note the shell porch on the left.

PUCKLECHURCH.

44166

The Village Green along the Westerleigh Road, with Parkfield Road off to the left. Pucklechurch House stands proudly in its own grounds, whilst the village school can be seen in the middle distance. Note the small finger-post on the right, with the arm pointing towards Parkfield and Henfield. c.1955.

In this view the trees are in their summer foliage, and part of the right-hand verge has given way to a lay-by. The road is marked out with white lines, and the direction sign is now on the Green. Other changes have occurred, but there is, coincidentally, a similar slant to the 1998 lamp-post as there was to the 1955 electric pole. Surely they were not put up by the same person??

The village school and neighbouring cottages as they appeared around 1906 in front of a rather badly worn grass triangle. A carter has stopped his wagon and stands alongside three children as they collectively pose for the camera.

The main Westerleigh Road has been re-aligned and widened, whilst the state of the grass seems to be as poor as it was ninety years ago. The cottages have been brought up-to-date, and the roof levels changed. Sadly the school has closed and will no longer enjoy the chatter of excited children sharing their educational experiences, as this part of the village life-blood is lost.

Copyright Lilywhite (1932) Ltd.
Sowerby Bridge.

VILLAGE GREEN, PUCKLECHURCH.   PKC.5.

Turning back towards the centre of the community, we approach the Village Green at the junction of the Parkfield and Westerleigh roads. Facing the Green is a group of houses and business premises, whilst on the right is part of the boundary wall surrounding Pucklechurch House. c.1931.

The modern road has been defined with the introduction of edging stones and white lines, leaving less to chance, whilst coping with todays modern traffic conditions. The left-hand wagon doorway has been replaced by a window, with the building now forming the Baker's Shop. The end-on houses on the right have been demolished.

VIEW SHOWING POST OFFICE, PUCKLECHURCH

W.J. Smith runs the Post Office and Newsagents, whilst his shop sports an array of enamelled advertising boards, plus no less than six dispensing machines offering a variety of goodies. Bigg's Blue tobacco can be purchased for 9d. (04p) an ounce. Opposite a garage business has been established and petrol can be purchased from a solitary hand-cranked pump.

The structure of the buildings remain basically the same, although the garage has opened up with a forecourt. The road is full of cars, as customers shop to suit their convenience. No longer is the Post Office festooned with enamel signs, whilst the opposite general store has received a modern shop front.

By stepping along the road past the shop on the left, we obtain this 1906 view of the Congregational Chapel. Frozen in time are two smartly dressed young ladies in their summer Sunday best, as they stroll along the road to avoid the dust of the earth foot-path. Just around the corner a group of young lads sit on the gate step contemplating exactly what to do with their time.

For structural safety reasons the chapel, which had its foundation stone laid on the 11 June 1845, had to be demolished during May 1991. All that now remains of the original building is the back wall, the boundary wall, plus the gate and its supporting posts, whilst the vestry is now used as the Congregational Church.

Leaving Pucklechurch on the Abson road at the junction with the road leading to Hinton. A large elm tree dominates the area as it spreads its shade across the road in this lovely summer view of around 1908, when it was quite safe for a group of children in their Sunday best to be asked by the photographer to straddle the road. Note the window boxes full of flowers.

The road over the years has been widened and the grass island at the junction removed, for the convenience of the motor car. The house on the right has gone, whilst opposite there have been a number of structural changes made to the cottage. No longer would it be safe to ask children or anyone else to have their photograph taken in the middle of the road.

ABSON CHURCH.

The only old commercial picture yet discovered of Abson is the ubiquitous one of the church. This view of St. James is taken from a card postally used on the 29 September 1916, and shows its Early English style of architecture, the chancel; the nave, and the South porch.

With the passage of time the trees surrounding the church-yard have grown, to the extent that it is now not possible to replicate the opposite view without their over-hanging branches framing the shot. However, this is the best shot of the embattled West tower which contains six bells.

High Street, Wick.

12634.

As we approach Wick along the A420 and, turn into the High Street, we pass the *Carpenter's Arms* on the left, whilst just beyond, the road on four arches, crosses the River Boyd before it starts to climb through the older parts of the village. On the left there are still a number of open fields yet to be built upon. c.1906/7.

The *Carpenter's Arms* remains much the same over the years, but the volume of traffic does not, as cars and lorries rush over the river despite the introduction of traffic calming measures. In doing so they also pass the spot where just over 100 years ago a certain Mr. James Ricketts met with a violent end having been robbed and then stabbed to death.

VIEW OF MAIN STREET, WICK.

Frozen in time around 1903 are two ladies having a 'gossip' whilst a man waits patiently by; a pony in harness grazes the grass bank; a wheel-barrow is being pushed along the middle of the road; three young men share one bicycle whilst, striding purposefully towards the photographer, is a smart business man wearing a Homburg and carrying a gladstone bag; could he be the local Doctor?

The garden trees have grown and now shield the view of the houses on the left. Opposite, the rank of cottages have been modernized, as has the road and the right-hand pedestrian way. Certainly it would no longer be safe to push a wheel-barrow along the middle of the road.

On through the village, we come across the *Rose and Crown Inn* basking in the summer sunshine of yester-year. This Inn was established more than 200 years ago and, it was here, during 1783, that John Gully, perhaps Wick's most famous son, was born. As a young man in need of money he took to bare-knuckle fighting and twice defended his title of Pugilist Champion of all England.

The external structure of the *Rose and Crown Inn* remains basically the same. The sign has been moved nearer the road, whilst the boundary between the grounds of the Inn and the roadway have been formally defined. Electricity is now carried under-ground, with the road illuminated by modern sodium lighting.

A view looking back down the hill with houses and the village school (built in 1854) on the right. A group of children peer at the photographer from the entrance to the playground, including at the front, a young man in breeches. At the bottom of the High Street can be seen the frontage of the *Carpenter's Arms.* Beyond, Naishcombe Hill is devoid of houses. c.1908.

The school building, but alas not the school itself, remain, but the adjoining houses have been completely rebuilt and modernized. Heavy lorries thunder by on their way to and from the motorway, and we no longer have the pastoral scene of yester-year.

The village sub-Post Office and Stationers with the local postman just about to go on his rounds. A King & Co. haulage wagon is about to breast the hill, whilst a smartly dressed man, sporting a boater, sits on an open carriage and pair. At the entrance to the timber/wheelwrights yard is a horse-drawn delivery van. An interesting snap-shot of Wick around 1912.

The old Post Office has now been converted into a private house. A parking bay has been constructed on the right, and traffic flows by as a young lady delivers the local evening paper amongst the hustle of the 'nineties'.

View of Main Street, Wick.

The Tabernacle United Reformed Church, which was built in 1837, stands in all its glory on a bright summers day around 1903. Nearest the camera, a mother is, with her two young children, about to negotiate the after perils of horse-drawn traffic. Her eldest daughter is wearing a large sun-hat whilst, beyond, is a group of fashionably-dressed young people on what might be a Sunday School event.

A large tree has grown over the years in an adjacent garden, preventing a full sided view of the chapel being taken, but basically the structure, now 160 years old, remains the same. Ponderous traffic lumbers along the main street, bringing in its wake, many changes which just could not have been contemplated by those who stand in the opposite picture.

Stephen Page stands proudly outside of his shop, being the purveyor of groceries, fabrics, and cloth to the locality. No doubt many other items were also sold, as indicated by the various advertising boards around the shop. Garden walls neatly separate the property from the pavement, all that appears to be missing are Mr. Page's customers.

The garden walls have gone, the background trees have thickened, and Wick Stores now sell a much wider selection of products than in the days of Mr. Page. Hot and cold snacks, drinks, ice creams and pasties all cry out to be purchased as the shop gears itself to meet the demands of today.

As the main part of the village is left behind, one of the last properties in Wick is Pool Farm, seen in this picture around 1903. The Ivy clad farm is situated on the curve of the Bath Road, as it swings round on its way to Lansdown and the City of Bath.

Today's scene has radically changed, with Pool Farm no longer covered in Ivy but, more noticeable, is the orientation of the road pattern. The road to the left of the Farm still takes the travellers to Lansdown, but for those heading for Chippenham, the A420 boldly strikes a route to take the traveller up over Tog Hill.

It seems as though the whole of Westerleigh have turned out to honour their dead of the First World War, as the memorial is dedicated 15 May 1920.

WESTERLEIGH WAR MEMORIAL, DEDICATION DAY, 15.5.1920. (Dowsing.)

Although a similar view has already been included, it was felt that it contained sufficient additional interest to merit its own inclusion. c.1911.

PUCKLECHURCH.

JUST A GLIMPSE

One of the very few postcards yet found of Dyrham Village, a view that was probably taken around 1923.

DYRHAM

All of the pictures in this, and the other 'Then & Now" books are available from the Author, in whole plate size (8" x 10"), both framed or unframed. Should anyone have any old photographs of the areas covered from which copies can be taken please contact me by writing or by telephone. (0117) 9323007.